T0061249

Contents

DISCUSSION GUIDE · PERSONAL STUDY · SCRIPTURE REFLECTION

NO ONE
DRIFTS INTO
SPIRITUAL
TRANSFORMATION.

John Ortberg

WE WOULD LIKE TO THANK:

Kris Kile, whose wisdom and labor is reflected throughout this entire guide. Without Kris's contributions, this series would not be what it is.

Jeff, for his ability to help us make this guide less informational and more conversational.

Jesse and his team at OX Creative, for the beautifully creative ways that they shaped the look and feel of this project.

Dean, for his courage, friendship, and sacrificial financial partnership.

CORE Ministries, Inc.
PO Box 93007
Austin TX 78709

COREUNITES.COM

WE ARE EXCITED YOU CHOSE TO BE A PART OF THIS JOURNEY.

We have been working with men in stadiums, arenas, churches, businesses, and homes for decades and can sum up what we have seen as their biggest battles in two words: *Isolation* and *Disqualification*.

- **Isolation: "If you knew how messed up some of my life is, you wouldn't want to have anything to do with me."**
- **Disqualification: "If you knew how messed up some of my life is, you wouldn't want me to have anything to do with you."**

The passion behind CORE is to create spaces where men have permission to be real. Spaces where men discover they are not alone with the kind of doubts and fears they face. Spaces where they have like-minded brothers who are there with them.

In spite of what our culture might tell us, **life was not designed to figure things out on our own.** When Jesus came to earth to start a revolution, he did so by gathering a small band of **ordinary men.**

OVERVIEW

These men had their own unique backgrounds, diverse occupations, and individual personalities. It was alongside one another that Jesus would orchestrate learning environments that would change them into the most powerful transformative community in the history of the world.

Together, these men went from being self-centered individuals to united powerhouses that forever changed the course of history. Jesus didn't just teach them wonderful truths. He modeled, coached, and empowered them on what it took to make those truths become a living reality in the challenging world in which they lived. Please hear this when we say, "Jesus is still forming and empowering communities today."

Our hope is that this 5-session small group experience is the beginning of a journey that transforms your group into this type of community.

Here are the basic elements we have prepared for you:

5 SHORT FILMS

We believe in the power of story. The 5 films connected with Series 1 are stories of real people facing real life challenges.

5-PART DISCUSSION GUIDE

We believe in the power of community. This guide will help facilitate small group interaction in a way that creates connection around things that matter.

5-PART PERSONAL STUDY AND SCRIPTURE REFLECTION

We believe in the power of personal study and reflection. This gives the opportunity, between group meetings, to move the ideas from the film and discussion into deeper understanding and growth.

GROUP DYNAMICS

COMBINED WITH THE FILMS, THE 5-SESSION GROUP DISCUSSION IS DESIGNED TO MAXIMIZE INTERACTION, CONNECTION AND MEANINGFUL CONVERSATIONS.

We've intentionally made this guide as straightforward as possible. Please know that each of these simple steps are specifically designed to help create maximum impact for you and your group. With that in mind, we encourage you to trust the process by following each step along with its suggested time frame.

CORE GROUP TIME CONSISTS OF:

1. Opening Prayer. Surrendering time and hearts to God's leading.

2. Check In. Discussing past week's issues, progress, and challenges.

3. Watch Film. Viewing together a 10- to 14-minute real-life story.

4. Discussion. Sharing personal impressions and thoughts about the film.

5. Next Steps. Discussing a measurable step that can be taken this coming week.

6. Personal Study Preview. Brief look at this week's personal study.

7. Closing Prayer. Asking for God's guidance and strength for the week ahead.

Each meeting together will serve as an opportunity to connect with each other, get real, build trust, and consider the important issues in the lives of everyone in your group.

IDEAL GROUP SIZE & TIME FRAME

An ideal small group size is 5–7. If the group is too small and somebody does not come or drops out, you can lose the collective perspective and encouragement a group can bring. If it is too large, you lose the opportunity for everyone to fully participate and build trust. If your group is larger, you can break into smaller groups for the discussion time. If you are meeting as a large group, we strongly encourage you keep the smaller groups together throughout your 5 sessions.

An ideal time frame for your group is 90 minutes. Of course, if your group decides, you can meet for longer or shorter periods. We recommend not meeting for less than 60 minutes. The suggested meeting agenda we have provided is based on the 90-minute time frame. If you meet longer or shorter, adjust accordingly.

Note that our language throughout is "each week." We find a lot of groups meet every other week. This can work great as well. For relational continuity we do not recommend meeting once a month.

GROUP FACILITATOR

We have consistently seen the #1 common denominator for most effective small groups is having one individual who is motivated to "owning" the group's formation, logistics, and reminders for the full 5 weeks. This will go a long way in seeing the group stay consistent and finish strong. Many times, that same guy guides the group through the discussion, but that is not always the case. The main responsibilities for an effective group facilitator are:

- Recruits men to join him in a 5-session small-group experience together.
- Makes sure everyone gets a study guide.
- Makes sure the meeting place and film watching portion are good to go.
- Communicates meeting time reminders and encouragement between gatherings.

MEETING LOGISTICS

The group dynamic is designed around watching a short film together each time you meet. This will require having the means to play the films and access to a proper screen and sound system. In choosing the meeting place, the fewer distractions you have, the greater the chance for open discussion. Some churches host larger gatherings of men who sit around individual tables. They all watch the film together and participate in all the discussion time at their tables. If you do this, we encourage you to keep the same guys at each table each week in order to build trust.

FIRST SESSION ORIENTATION

Please be sure that your group goes over the Sharing and Group Guidelines in the first session and has a chance to ask any clarification questions. Have the group agree to commit to these Guidelines. They are simple yet designed to enhance your experience together.

OVERVIEW

Here is how everything fits together for this series.

- Each meeting you will go through the Group Discussion Guide, watch a film, and discuss personal relevance and application.
- In between each session, you will go through the Personal Study and Scripture Reflection to process the major theme of that film and think more deeply on supporting Scriptures.
- At the next meeting you will have an opportunity to discuss what you discovered, worked through, and what stood out to you during your Personal Study and Scripture Reflection time.

We encourage your group to consider at least one "off the script" meeting (i.e., BBQ, movie, sporting event, games, cards, etc.). We lay these out more fully at coreunites.com/whatsnext.

In the first session together, please **read out loud these guidelines** for everyone to have an opportunity to discuss and agree to.

GROUP DISCUSSION GUIDELINES

We believe that if you can stay within the riverbanks of these four guidelines, you will maximize a positive small experience for everyone.

1. Personalize, Not Sermonize. What does the specific issue being discussed mean for my life, my concerns, my dreams versus the need to give additional insights to others? The courage to speak from personal transparency contributes significantly to everyone in your group. Speak more from the "I", "my", "me" and NOT the "you" and "we" position. This can be difficult for those of us who are teachers or those who wish to be seen as insightful.

2. Be Brief. Be thoughtful not to dominate discussion time. Think in terms of 1-2 minutes each time you share. If you know you are someone who loves to share, discipline yourself to actively listen. If you have something that needs more time to unpack, make a request to discuss it later. Being brief can be difficult for those of us who externally process versus those who internalize thoughts before speaking.

3. Encourage, Not Fix. We honor courageous authenticity. We discourage group counsel or correction. We need to take responsibility for our own actions, results, and experiences. This can be difficult for those of us who are counselors or "fixers."

4. Maintain Confidentiality. Keep everything shared confidential. Do not repeat it to ANYONE outside your CORE group, including spouses or close friends. This can be difficult for those of us who don't highly value what it means to be a trusted confidante.

SMALL GROUP COURTESTY "101s"

- If you are going to be late or absent, call someone in your group to inform them.
- No cellphone use during the meeting, unless permission is asked at the beginning of the meeting.
- Don't leave the group permanently without speaking to your group about it.

There are **5 films** that go along with ***CORE** for Men: Transformed.* These are a central component to the small-group experience.

ADDITIONAL SMALL GROUP BEST PRACTICES

Here are some additional small group dynamic insights that will be beneficial for your CORE group to be aware of:

- The purpose of a CORE group is to encourage us to think and discuss from a personal heart perspective. When the film ends, go directly into the first discussion question, "What part of _____ story or sharing stuck out to you?"

- The CORE discussion time is a simple invitation to be real. No posturing required. "Being real" can mean different things to different people. So, be respectful of each other and embrace what "being real" means for them. That includes not making anyone feel like they have to share something personal. When everyone in a group feels like they can relax and be themselves, it's surprising how God will help open up the group's interaction over time.

- Interrupt any tendency you feel to judge another. We get enough of that already.

- Avoid being an "advice giver." If someone in the group wants input or feedback, let them ask for it. If you have input you want to offer, ask permission to give it. Feel free to not grant permission to someone to give input if you are not ready to hear it from them.

- Do not shut down someone who may choose to use strong language or express raw emotion in describing their perspective and experience (i.e., swearing, raising voice, etc.).

- Be respectful of the time frames included in the meeting agenda for each week. As briefly discussed earlier in our Group Guidelines, a common problem is the tendency of one guy to dominate the group time. If someone is going over on time, after the meeting, respectfully remind them of the guidelines. If they persist, kindly remind them during the group time out of respect for the rest of the group.

- There will be some very good and open conversations in the "Check In" and "Discussion" time. Make sure you leave yourselves a little room for the "Next Steps," "Personal Study Preview," and "Closing Prayer" time.
- The current culture is high on talking but slow on doing. When you purposefully give time to ask, "What specific step am I going to take this week?" it can move your group into new levels of discovery and breakthrough. This also gives everyone something specific to pray for one another during the week.
- In your first time together, write down everyone's name in this guide and during the week, take a moment to pray for each guy by name. It doesn't have to be a long prayer. Watch what happens to your own heart toward the guys in your group when you do this. It's pretty awesome to see how your heart changes toward the group.
- When you discuss how your previous week's "Next Steps" and "Personal Study" went, this is a "no shame zone." Growth and new habits take time. Empathy, encouragement, and patience go a long way toward building the kind of environment that will surface root issues and facilitate breakthrough.
- Pay attention to the men in your group. If it seems like there might be a guy who would have an easier time opening up "one on one," look for an opportunity to grab a coffee or a bite to eat. These moments can be great for some guys.
- Finally, a great CORE group meeting, which takes time to evolve, has an ease and a flow to it. It is not a rigidly enforced agenda, but it is important to follow the established guidelines that allow enough time for each of the group elements.

LET'S GO!

IDENTITY

PROPAGANDA

GROUP DISCUSSION GUIDE (90 MINUTES)

OPENING PRAYER
Surrender your time and heart to God's leading.

CHECK IN (15 MINUTES—1–2 MINUTES PER PERSON)

1. Share your name.

2. Main reasons for wanting to be or continue in the group.

3. One thing you would like to get from participating in these next 5 sessions.

TOGETHER READ THE GUIDELINES ON PAGE 9. (15 MINUTES)
These are simple yet designed to enhance your group experience.

1. Does everyone in the group understand them?

2. Are there any clarification questions regarding any of the guidelines?

3. Can we commit to these as a group?

Note: Many of you are seeing this study guide for the first time. There is some foundational information in the Overview and Group Dynamics section that would be well worth reading before you meet again.

WATCH FILM (12 MINUTES)
Identity—Propaganda

GROUP DISCUSSION (35 MINUTES)
Be mindful of the need for everyone to have the opportunity to talk. Take 1–2 minutes each time you share.

1. What did you connect with in Propaganda's sharing?

2. What "norms about manhood" do you think are influencing what you believe about yourself? How does that contrast with what God says about you?

NEXT STEPS (10 MINUTES)

In light of today's discussion, what is one step you can take in your life or in your relationships this week? Something specific. Something measurable. Something the group can pray for during the week.

THE PURPOSE OF THE PERSONAL STUDY AND SCRIPTURE REFLECTION—READ OUT LOUD (2 MINUTES)

The Personal Study and Scripture Reflection section in this guide is included in each of the sessions. Taking time each week to do them can be one of the most important things you choose to do over these next 5 weeks. It is the difference between randomly throwing seed on the ground versus planting it deeply. Setting aside time for personal study and prayerful reflection is a new rhythm for many. Committing to this, along with showing up every week with your group, will strengthen your ability to drop old thoughts and habits and take on new ways to think and live.

PERSONAL STUDY EXCERPT—READ OUT LOUD (2 MINUTES)

What is identity? It's your perception of who you are, why you are that way, and what you do to sustain that perception.

Life and the cultures we are born into offer us one identity and this is the first set of identities we take on. It's like fish swimming in the water. The fish don't even think about water. It is just the environment they swim in. It is like the air we breathe. Air is what surrounds us. How often do you remind yourself to breathe? Not often, if at all. It's just the environment you were born into; you embraced it with your first breath and didn't give it another thought unless you were forced to.

This is how the identity we developed as children happened.

CLOSING PRAYER

Ask for God's guidance and strength for the week ahead.

CORE GROUP NOTES

Remember WHO YOU ARE man of God!

You ARE a chosen, forgiven, redeemed son of the Creator of the universe.

You ARE a commissioned minister of reconciliation.

You ARE co-heir with Christ to the kingdom of heaven.

And you ARE my brother.

In this film, Jason Petty, aka Propaganda, offers us a brilliant dissertation on identity, what forms it, what is our old identity, what is offered to us as a new identity, and how we transition from one to the other.

First, let's think about this for a few moments. What is identity? It's your perception of who you are, why you are that way, and what you do to sustain that perception.

Life and the cultures we are born into offer us one identity and this is the first set of identities we take on. It's like fish swimming in the water. The fish don't even think about water. It is just the environment they swim in. It is like the air we breathe. Air is what surrounds us. How often do you remind yourself to breathe? Not often, if at all. It's just the environment you were born into; you embraced it with your first breath and didn't give it another thought unless you were forced to.

This is how the identity we developed as children happened.

We just naturally, often automatically, took on points of view, beliefs and 'tribal affiliations' based on the primary influences in our lives.

For example, if you like sports, what are your favorite sports teams? What are your political beliefs? What are your points of view on racial matters?

Where you land on each of these matters has as much to do with the influences you had growing up as it does your own independent thinking.

Many of the "tribes" you are a part of now were automatically adopted, due to your place of origin, family of origin, geographical location of origin, and the experiences you had. Often, we instinctually choose our preferences without much thought. And, then, somewhere along the way, we may start questioning these preferences.

Let's take a look at how Propaganda described this identity challenge. Consider his thoughts in light of how you may have built your own identity.

He noticed how he had formed his original identity growing up:

What he thought it meant to be a man . . .

"We were in this Latino neighborhood and what I knew from Latino men is, yo . . . men work, like that's what you do. They work long hours, hard hours. That's what men do."

"So, if you ain't working, you ain't a real man."

The allure and fallacy of the self-made man . . .

"I don't like the idea that somebody had to do something for me for me to get where I am. But it's such a dumb thing to not like because everything is like that, somebody did something for you."

You are what you do . . .

"I have a profession where our value is quantified by ticket sales and album sales. If you have friends that are killing it . . . doing better than you . . . oftentimes you feel like 'dang, like what am I doing? What am I doing wrong?' It starts becoming like super competition with buddies. And I think that's been such a hindrance in the sense that sometimes it sparks jealousy . . . like envy toward people who are your loved ones."

REMEMBER WHO YOU ARE MAN OF GOD! YOU ARE A CHOSEN, FORGIVEN, REDEEMED SON OF THE CREATOR OF THE UNIVERSE. YOU ARE A COMMISSIONED MINISTER OF RECONCILIATION. YOU ARE CO-HEIR WITH CHRIST TO THE KINGDOM OF HEAVEN. AND YOU ARE MY BROTHER.

"The ramifications of thinking you are what you do . . .

"But when I feel like I'm not as good as them or the world doesn't think I'm as good as them, I stop pursuing the fullness of who I am, and I'm just overwhelmed with who they are."

Building a new identity . . .

"So, what it means for my identity to be on purpose is that I don't have to see myself from a deficit model. A lot of times as dudes, we're like 'Yo, I worked hard. I struggled. You know I failed at this.' So, it's like you're starting from a deficit. And then mistakes happen. We look back like 'I shouldn't have done this or shouldn't have done that.' Again, it's a deficit. But if I say no, this is on purpose, I'm not starting from a deficit. I'm starting from purpose. Then moving forward is not reactionary or in regret. It's moving from design. If I can see my identity as a design, like I'm black on purpose, and I'm from LA on purpose . . . I know what I've gone through was on purpose. Like God was painting something bigger."

"When I understand my life is that, then . . . . Of course, it isn't to excuse mistakes or things that I had no control over. I don't see those as victim inducing. I see this as by design."

Expressing this new identity . . .

"I realize a lot of my definition of manhood was just misogyny and patriarchy, which is oppressive. And I've learned now as a married man and a grownup how quickly I can humble myself . . . Esteeming others higher than myself . . . leveraging power and privilege for others.

"For me now that is the mark of manhood. If I want to lead, then lead by service . . . lead through submission. Ultimately this is the call for all of us, but specifically as a dude, given the context of our culture, I want to lead by not trying to gain power but trying to lay it down. Now I feel like that's manhood."

Transitioning from the old identity to the new identity . . .

"Forgiveness was the Father stooping down. And I think that that's such a challenge to our concept of manhood of you working to get yours. You get where you get because you grinded. That's the way I thought. What man meant was work. Nobody hands you anything. Everybody has the same 24 hours. I just need to make mine be 32. You know what I'm saying? But forgiveness came out of the heart of the Father—not because of the actions of the receiver, which points us to the adoption part, which means you had no hand in this; but both of those things—they immediately humble and they level the playing field and they say, 'You know this is the action. We are receivers, rather than givers.'"

We close with this final thought for you to consider from Propaganda . . .

"I think at the end of the day I would challenge men to challenge their norms. Question things that you figured were set in stone as far as our definitions of manhood, of strength, and beauty of leadership. I think when you're willing to really question and deconstruct, you can reconstruct into a better configuration. Sometimes winning is losing. Sometimes leading is to serve. It is to be humble and [realize that] identity doesn't come solely from our experiences, but from our Maker."

PERSONAL STUDY NOTES

SCRIPTURE REFLECTION

 **PERSONAL STUDY QUESTIONS**

Some things become clearer when you take the time to actually write down your thoughts. Though it is not a familiar practice for many, consider taking a few minutes with each of these 4 questions:

1. Consider some of your identities you derived from the culture, location, and family you were born into. How many aspects of your identity can you list as you consider this?

2. Consider your attitude toward others who are in "tribes" that differ or oppose the group identities that you have adopted. Think specifics . . . your attitude toward those who have different points of view politically, religiously, opposing sports team fans, different ethnicities. What do you notice?

3. Reread this opening quote and consider how this is a better description of who you really are:

   - Remember WHO YOU ARE man of God!
   - You ARE a chosen, forgiven, redeemed son of the Creator of the universe.
   - You ARE a commissioned minister of reconciliation.
   - You ARE co-heir with Christ to the kingdom of heaven.
   - And you ARE my brother.

4. Have I addressed my "Next Steps" that I shared with my CORE group? If not, what is keeping me from stepping out and addressing it? What's my next step?

SCRIPTURE REFLECTION PRACTICE

We encourage you to consider the following Scripture passage over the course of this week in a prayerfully contemplative way. This simple process will help you engage not only your mind but also your heart. Consider focusing this week on the same Scripture below (Jeremiah 9:23–24) each day, using these principles:

- Be alert for a phrase or word that catches your attention. This could be in the form of a question on what it means or a new insight.
- Once during the week, read the verses aloud slowly.
- Once during the week, as you read the verses, pause along the way to use it to spark specific prayers to God.
- Finally, after reading the verses, pause to be thankful that "*it is God who works in you, both to will and to work for his good pleasure.*" **Philippians 2:13 (ESV)**

SCRIPTURE REFLECTION FOR SESSION 2: JEREMIAH 9:23–24 (ESV)

Thus says the LORD: "Let not the wise man boast in his wisdom,
let not the mighty man boast in his might,
let not the rich man boast in his riches,
but let him who boasts boast in this,
that he understands and knows me,
that I am the LORD who practices steadfast love, justice,
and righteousness in the earth.
For in these things I delight, declares the LORD."

SCRIPTURE REFLECTION NOTES

TRANSFORMATION

WILLIE ALFONSO

GROUP DISCUSSION GUIDE (90 MINUTES)

OPENING PRAYER

Surrender your time and heart to God's leading.

CHECK IN (20 MINUTES—2–3 MINUTES PER PERSON)

Be mindful of the need for everyone to have the opportunity to talk. Take 1–2 minutes each time you share.

1. How has your week gone? Family? Work?

2. What kind of progress or challenges did you have with your "Next Steps" from last session?

3. How was your Personal Study and Scripture Reflection time this week? What is resonating? What is not working?

WATCH FILM (11 MINUTES)
Transformation—Willie Alfonso

GROUP DISCUSSION (45 MINUTES)

1. Which part of Willie's story did you connect with?

2. Briefly share what was positive and negative about the relationship with your father/stepfather. How do you think that relationship impacted your life and decisions?

NEXT STEPS (10 MINUTES)
Be mindful of the need for everyone to have an opportunity to talk. Take 2–3 minutes each. Take notes and pray for each other's "Next Steps" during the week. As always, keep everything confidential.

In light of today's discussion, what is one step you can take in your life or in your relationships this week? Something specific. Something measurable. Something the group can pray for during the week.

PERSONAL STUDY EXCERPT—READ OUT LOUD (4 MINUTES)
Oftentimes we hear about a person's radical life-change, and it sounds almost too good to be true. We might even become envious of such a powerful story because we have a hard time seeing our own lives being changed in that way. It is easy to assume that a person's outward transformation is more glamorous and immediate than it really is.

All of us have a past that has shaped us. For better or worse we all have people and circumstances that have shaped how we see God, how we see ourselves, and how we see others. Our history, personality, and experiences have a way of convincing us of what is true—even when it's not. Graciously, God has given us His Word so that we can confidently know how to think, how to see, and how to live.

CLOSING PRAYER
Ask for God's guidance and strength during the week ahead.

WHAT LIES BEHIND US AND WHAT LIES BEFORE US ARE TINY MATTERS COMPARED TO WHAT LIES WITHIN US.

Ralph Waldo Emerson

CORE GROUP NOTES

◊ PERSONAL STUDY

Willie's story shows the power of God's redemptive grace, especially considering his upbringing. Today, Willie serves as the chaplain of the New York Yankees and is involved in serving God and others in a myriad of ways. But that's not how his story began.

Growing up, Willie endured tremendous suffering and rejection:

- He was abused by his violent father.
- He was abandoned by his father and mother.
- He was homeless, sleeping and eating on the streets of New York at 11 years old.
- He experienced deep rejection.
- He was a drug addict.
- He felt deep anger and bitterness toward his father.

And yet God rescued him from all of that.

Perhaps your background is not as dramatic as Willie's. Perhaps it's even worse. Regardless, we all experience loss, betrayal, and failure in some form or another. A harmful tendency we have in response to these hardships is to excuse, minimize, or dismiss them as not relevant or not a big deal. But they have influenced us just the same.

Willie recounted the persistence of a coworker who shared an alternative to the self-destructive path he was on. This man told Willie that there was forgiveness found in Jesus. Willie received the gift of God's grace and began learning how to live as an empowered follower of Jesus.

Oftentimes we hear about a person's radical life-change, and it sounds almost too good to be true. We might even become envious of such a powerful story because we have a hard time seeing our own lives being changed in that way. It is easy to assume that a person's outward transformation is more glamorous and immediate than it really is.

How does a life like Willie's change so radically? How did Willie get his life turned around?

Though there were many contributing factors, Willie says that it was the daily influence of God's Word that shaped this profound life-change. The Scriptures showed him a new way of addressing the challenges of his life and softened his heart so that he could see those challenges differently. Here's what Willie says about this:

"I love the Word of God. I think there's an eighteen-inch difference between what you believe here (in your head), and what you transfer here, to your heart. I read the Word of God just about every day.

"You know **Psalms 119** says, 'Thy word I have hidden in my heart so that I might not sin against God. I can't tell you how many times I read my Bible in the morning, went outside, and that day I ran into a struggle and that verse I read bailed me out.

"I had a guy cut me off not too long ago. I chased this dude down to the red light. I can't tell you what I was thinking. I wasn't chasing him to get him saved! And when I caught up to him, I told him, 'Roll your window down, my man.' Then I love how the truth of God comes. The Bible says at the moment of temptation God will always give you the way of escape. You know what God said? 'Yo stupid! What are you doing man? You're about to bang this thing up.'

"I make it my business to stay in the Word of God, and I also make it my business to hear God speak to me and respond right then.

"My father may have never told me he loved me, but my heavenly Father tells me every single day. 'Willie, you're special. I love you. I have something special for you to do that only you can do.'"

Willie shared one of the most important keys in experiencing a breakthrough in how you are living: He doesn't see reading Scripture as something he is supposed to do as a "good" Christian. He sees it in the same way a soldier would view his weapon. It gives him what he needs to face the challenges ahead.

A starting point is reading, reflecting, and declaring the truth of what God says is true about who we are. We are sons of the Creator of the universe. This understanding is the starting point of replacing old self-destructive habits with new ways of thinking and living.

Willie admits that this process is not finished and that he is continually being changed. But it's important that we have a clear view of how he is changing. It wasn't like he just prayed a prayer or snapped his fingers, and then became a changed man. Instead, just as Willie shared, it was how God's Word not only enabled him to see the ways he needed to change but gave him the strength and wisdom to carry out His divine purpose to make a difference in others.

- He embraced God's truth in Scripture and studied it.
- He reflected upon it.
- He applied it in his life.
- He allowed it to instruct, challenge, and encourage him.
- He applied discipline to this process. He became a disciple— a disciplined one.
- He embraced the possibility of being transformed by the renewing of his mind.
- He made his "Next Steps" to hear and obey.

Learning, examining and applying the truth of God from His Word is inwardly life-giving, and outwardly life-changing.

For the word of God is living and active, sharper than any two-edged sword, piercing to the division of soul and of spirit, of joints and of marrow, and discerning the thoughts and intentions of the heart.
Hebrews 4:12 (ESV)

Willie poured himself into studying and reflecting on Scripture. In doing so, he was replacing the lies of the corrupt culture that brought him up with the life-giving truth of God.

In obeying the Word of God:

- Willie replaced bitterness and rejection with forgiveness and acceptance.
- He replaced isolation with connected brotherhood.
- He replaced abandonment with community.
- He replaced using drugs with being freed by God and being used for His perfect purposes.
- He replaced self-centered survival with other-centered service.

All of us have a past that has shaped us. For better or worse we all have people and circumstances that have shaped how we see God, how we see ourselves, and how we see others. Our history, personality, and experiences have a way of convincing us of what is true, even when it's not. Graciously, God has given us His Word so that we can confidently know how to think, how to see, and how to live.

PERSONAL STUDY NOTES

SCRIPTURE REFLECTION

PERSONAL STUDY QUESTIONS

1. How did your relationship with your father influence how you are living out your life today?

2. Where do you need to exercise forgiveness for others in order to more fully experience freedom and God's forgiveness for you?

3. Have I addressed my action step that I shared with my CORE group? If not, what is keeping me from stepping out and addressing it? What's my next step?

SCRIPTURE REFLECTION PRACTICE

We encourage you to consider the following Scripture passage over the course of this week in a prayerfully contemplative way. This simple process will help you engage not only your mind but also your heart. Consider focusing this week on the same Scripture below (Psalm 119:9–16) each day, using these principles:

- Be alert for a phrase or word that catches your attention. This could be in the form of a question on what it means or a new insight.
- Once during the week, read the verses aloud slowly.
- Once during the week, as you read the verses, pause along the way to use it to spark specific prayers to God.
- Finally, after reading the verses, pause to be thankful that *"it is God who works in you, both to will and to work for his good pleasure."* **Philippians 2:13 (ESV)**

SCRIPTURE REFLECTION FOR SESSION 2:
PSALM 119:9–16 (ESV)

How can a young man keep his way pure?
By guarding it according to your word.
With my whole heart I seek you;
let me not wander from your commandments!
I have stored up your word in my heart,
that I might not sin against you.
Blessed are you, O LORD;
teach me your statutes!
With my lips I declare
all the rules of your mouth.
In the way of your testimonies I delight
as much as in all riches.
I will meditate on your precepts
and fix my eyes on your ways.
I will delight in your statutes;
I will not forget your word.

SCRIPTURE REFLECTION NOTES

BROTHERHOOD

SAM & EMMANUEL ACHO

GROUP DISCUSSION GUIDE (90 MINUTES)

OPENING PRAYER

Surrender your time and heart to God's leading.

CHECK IN (20 MINUTES—-2–3 MINUTES PER PERSON)

Be mindful of the need for everyone to have the opportunity to talk. Take 1–2 minutes each time you share.

1. How has your week gone? Family? Work?

2. What kind of progress or challenges did you have with your "Next Steps" from last session?

3. How was your Personal Study and Scripture Reflection time this week? What is resonating? What is not working?

WATCH FILM (11 MINUTES)
Brotherhood—Sam & Emmanuel Acho

DISCUSSION (45 MINUTES)

1. What part of the Acho's story did you connect with?

2. Sam said he regrets not opening up to his brother about the things he messed up in. What are the reasons we have that keep us from opening up to those close to us?

3. What can we do as a group to increase the level of authenticity and connection with each other?

NEXT STEPS (10 MINUTES)
Be mindful of the need for everyone to have an opportunity to talk. Take 2–3 minutes each. Take notes and pray for each other's "Next Steps" during the week. As always, keep everything confidential.

In light of today's discussion, what is one step you can take in your life or in your relationships this week? Something specific. Something measurable. Something the group can pray for during the week.

PERSONAL STUDY EXCERPT—READ OUT LOUD (4 MINUTES)
There was a reason Jesus picked men from vastly different backgrounds.

Do you think Matthew, the "sell-out" tax collector and Simon the anti-tax zealot had some interesting water cooler conversations? It certainly wasn't a political alliance that created their common bond.

What they had in common was a willingness to pay a price to follow Jesus. A willingness to be challenged to the core of their old identities and loyalties to share their singular most important identity—being followers of Jesus. They had lots of hang-ups and self-interests. But this singular common commitment made them a formidable group. One that the greatest powers on earth could not and would not stop.

CLOSING PRAYER

Ask for God's guidance and strength during the week ahead.

CORE GROUP NOTES

Your CORE group is designed to help facilitate a "brotherhood" connection with those in your group. This group serves as an opportunity to be completely open and honest. It is a relationship committed to addressing issues that can have a significant impact on your life and those around you.

What's the number one quality you want in your CORE group? It's not common life stage. Not common education. Not common economic status. Not common ethnicity. Not common political bias. Not common spiritual maturity. Then what is it?

Common purpose! Are you all after the same thing?

If you have the same ultimate goal, then the other differences actually work for you. They give you different perspectives to help one another achieve the same end goal. There was a reason Jesus picked men from vastly different backgrounds.

Do you think Matthew, the "sell-out" tax collector and Simon the anti-tax zealot had some interesting water cooler conversations? It certainly wasn't a political alliance that created their common bond.

What they had in common was a willingness to pay a price to follow Jesus. A willingness to be challenged to the core of their old identities and loyalties to share their singular most important identity—being followers of Jesus. They had lots of hang-ups and self-interests. But this singular common commitment made them a formidable group. One that the greatest powers on earth could not and would not stop.

Are you willing to share the good, the bad, and the ugly in order to help your CORE group overcome old ways and beliefs? To be open to embrace one another's vulnerabilities with encouragement and grace?

It takes courage to be real, rather than trying to mask with half-truths, denial, minimizing, or lying. It creates an intimacy and connection that enables you to share what causes suffering in your life and what you are challenged with. We all have that. Vulnerability can be life-giving, enabling you to share with others who need it.

> **"BROTHERHOOD" IS ONE OF THE GREATEST ENVIRONMENTS TO EXPERIENCE THE KIND OF TRANSFORMATION YOU DESIRE.**

In the film, Sam shares a regret in his relationship with his brother: "I've missed the boat, in my opinion, in being Emmanuel's brother, for example, his relationships with women—and even in my mistakes, I didn't really share that with him because if I jacked up, made a mistake, and know he knows, that might give him permission to do the same. So, I most wanted to maintain this perception of being a perfect older brother—which probably hurt him more than helped him.

"In my mind, the only way an example would be helpful is if it were perfect.

"I wanted him to think I have it all together and you can have it all together, too. Which no one does. There's nobody in the world who does. But I wanted him to view it that way. I think if I would have been more transparent with him about my failures and my struggles and stuff that I'm going through daily, it probably would have helped him more. The reality is that I'm still trying to figure out Sam (who I am)."

Sam goes on to say, "Just be yourself, stop trying to fit into this situation or that situation and be liked by these guys or by those guys or be cool, look cool, and just be who you are. I love the fact that he and I have such a close relationship, because not a lot of brothers have that. I don't feel like I have to hide or pretend. I live and die for relationships. It's like my brother coming to Chicago to hang out with me or me going to Austin and us kicking it. He's more reserved, just let him do his thing on his phone, and I'm like, hey, tell me about your life."

MY BEST FRIEND IS THE ONE WHO BRINGS OUT THE BEST IN ME.

Henry Ford

"Tell me about this girl you've been dating. Tell me about football. Tell me about what's going on. What is God teaching you?"

Consider this question. When you heard Sam share how he hid some things from his brother, did you think less of him? His honesty was refreshing to hear, wasn't it? For the vast majority of us, not only did we not think less of Sam, but we actually appreciated him more! Why is that? Because there is something very powerful when a friend is willing to open up about personal weakness with the hope to overcome. It brings the best out of us on so many levels.

Just like each of us, Sam and Emmanuel are learning the dynamics of true brotherhood. While they are brothers from the same family, these dynamics hold true for all friendships, whether related by blood or not.

Your CORE group might be a God-given opportunity for you to begin trusting one another with issues that you've been struggling to figure out on your own. It is up to you though. It will take an act of courage to lay yourself bare like this. It is your choice. If you don't think it wise to discuss an issue with the entire group, then consider whom in the group you can share it with.

"Brotherhood" is one of the greatest environments to experience the kind of transformation you dream of. It is designed to help free us from self-centered, isolated, secret living. **It is in brotherhood that you can learn one of the most powerful and life-giving experiences—wanting someone else's breakthrough to be as important to you as if it were your own.** It's what Jesus modeled for us. It is how we were originally designed to live.

Our culture is so isolating. The isolation that most live in is suffocating. It breeds desperation and hopelessness, a toxic combination.

The belief that others aren't struggling with similar issues makes us want to lie and hide our true selves. In our culture we are trained to speak as if we are confident, thriving, and healthy. Yet underneath the surface we know that we often aren't those things. We need to know others and be known by others, but we rarely know how to do that. Ralph Waldo Emerson said, "The glory of friendship is not the outstretched hand, nor the kindly smile, nor the joy of companionship. It is the spiritual inspiration that comes to one when he discovers that someone else believes in him and is willing to trust him."

Your CORE Group Dynamics are designed to create a deep sense of friendship with each other over time. It doesn't happen overnight. And our hope and prayer is that your group continues beyond the ten weeks of this particular foundational season.

Make the practice of "brotherhood" a mainstay in your life.

A very simple way to go deeper with this is to review the CORE Group Dynamics section at the front of this guide. Think of these methods as ways of being with each other that create opportunities to be real and connect so that you can help one another experience personal breakthroughs. This is one of the ultimate expressions of love.

"Love is unselfishly choosing for another's highest good." C.S. Lewis

PERSONAL STUDY NOTES

SCRIPTURE REFLECTION

**PERSONAL
STUDY
QUESTIONS**

1. What are you currently struggling with and what would you like to invite your CORE group to support you in?

2. Where can you be more effective in supporting your CORE group?

3. Have I addressed my "Next Steps" that I shared with my CORE group? If not, what is keeping me from stepping out and addressing it? What's my next step?

SCRIPTURE REFLECTION PRACTICE

We encourage you to consider the following Scripture passage over the course of this week in a prayerfully contemplative way. This simple process will help you engage not only your mind but also your heart. Consider focusing this week on the same Scripture below (Philippians 1:27–2:2) each day, using these principles:

- Be alert for a phrase or word that catches your attention. This could be in the form of a question on what it means or a new insight.
- Once during the week, read the verses aloud slowly.
- Once during the week, as you read the verses, pause along the way to use it to spark specific prayers to God.
- Finally, after reading the verses, pause to be thankful that *"it is God who works in you, both to will and to work for his good pleasure."* **Philippians 2:13 (ESV)**

SCRIPTURE REFLECTION FOR SESSION 3:
PHILIPPIANS 1:27–2:2 (ESV)

Only let your manner of life be worthy of the gospel of Christ, so that whether I come and see you or am absent, I may hear of you that you are standing firm in one spirit, with one mind striving side by side for the faith of the gospel, and not frightened in anything by your opponents.

This is a clear sign to them of their destruction, but of your salvation, and that from God. For it has been granted to you that for the sake of Christ you should not only believe in him but also suffer for his sake, engaged in the same conflict that you saw I had and now hear that I still have.

So if there is any encouragement in Christ, any comfort from love, any participation in the Spirit, any affection and sympathy, complete my joy by being of the same mind, having the same love, being in full accord and of one mind.

SCRIPTURE REFLECTION NOTES

CHOICES

JERRY QUIROZ

GROUP DISCUSSION GUIDE (90 MINUTES)

OPENING PRAYER

Surrender your time and heart to God's leading.

CHECK IN (20 MINUTES—2–3 MINUTES PER PERSON)

Be mindful of the need for everyone to have the opportunity to talk.
Take 1–2 minutes each time you share.

1. How has your week gone? Family? Work?

2. What kind of progress or challenges did you have with your "Next Steps" from last session?

3. How was your Personal Study and Scripture Reflection time this week? What is resonating? What is not working?

CHOICES

WATCH FILM (10 MINUTES)
Choices—Jerry Quiroz

GROUP DISCUSSION (45 MINUTES)

1. What part of Jerry's story did you connect with?

2. What hard decisions are you currently facing? What do you need to help you with this?

NEXT STEPS (10 MINUTES)
Be mindful of the need for everyone to have an opportunity to talk. Take 2–3 minutes each. Take notes and pray for each other's "Next Steps" during the week. As always, keep everything confidential.

In light of today's discussion, what is one step you can take in your life or in your relationships this week? Something specific. Something measurable. Something the group can pray for during the week.

PERSONAL STUDY EXCERPT—READ OUT LOUD (5 MINUTES)
We, like Jason Bourne, have let the wounds of life cause us to forget who we are. We need others to remind us of who we really are. It's not about giving endless advice. It's not about judging. It's not about shaming. It's not about avoiding. It's not about minimizing or dismissing.

Instead, it's about loving, being honest, transparent, real, and encouraging. We all struggle. To deny it is vanity and willful blindness. Having fellow wounded healers alongside us is how God rolls best.

Don't go it alone. You may stumble. If you do, pick yourself up and go again. Moment by moment, we choose. And those choices determine the trajectory of our lives.

CLOSING PRAYER
Ask for God's guidance and strength during the week ahead.

CORE GROUP NOTES

Jerry's story is a story of grace. Out of God's kindness and His love, He intervened while Jerry rebelled. This is what God does. It's the story of the gospel. Even though we haven't deserved it, God already has a plan in place to save us from ourselves. Life can get messy, but in Jerry's story we see that God's passion is to rescue us by providing an alternative.

Have you gotten to a place where you've given up hope that God will ever change some part of you? Is there some insecurity, temperament, or behavior that, at this point, you're just so accustomed to, that you're now convinced, "This is just who I am"?

But you are never too old, too rebellious, or too hopeless for God to intervene. This is one of the most consistent narratives in the entire Bible: God transforms people. He gives us new longings. He gives us new desires. He changes our hearts, which changes the way we live. Whatever your story is, our hope is that you see that God has the desire and the power to change you.

We cannot emphasize enough that those in your CORE group are a valuable resource in this transformation. Jerry's friend, Nathan, was that resource to him. In the film, Jerry recounts after he confessed his lying and cheating to his wife:

"I felt like everything that was holding us just got torn. And I prayed to God, and I said, 'God, you told me to say these things, so now, where are you?' For my marriage, this was the lowest point. I went to seek help at our church and our young adult ministry pastor, Nathan, was there. I let him know what just happened. Nathan was a great support during this difficult time. The love and forgiveness from God came through being around other men of God who imparted that identity in me. I found this allowed me to fully receive forgiveness as a son. This is the beauty of friendship."

RESCUE IS THE CONSTANT PATTERN OF GOD'S ACTIVITY.

Francis Frangipane

We, like Jason Bourne, have let the wounds of life cause us to forget who we are. We need others to remind us who we really are. It's not about giving endless advice. It's not about judging. It's not about shaming. It's not about avoiding. It's not about minimizing or dismissing.

Instead it's about loving, being honest, transparent, real, and encouraging. We all struggle. To deny it is vanity and willful blindness. Having fellow wounded healers alongside us is how God rolls best.

Now, all of these descriptions of God's restorative work in our lives is energizing and refreshing. But you have a responsibility in this work. You must be willing to get real about your life, as it currently is. This is something we see in Jerry's story.

Jerry's life came to a crossroads. God opened his eyes so that Jerry could see how his dream of becoming a star soccer player had become a self-destructive idol.

Tim Keller gives some helpful insight, **"What is an idol? It is anything more important to you than God, anything that absorbs our heart and imagination more than God, anything you seek to give you what only God can give."**

Anything can become an idol for you.

- Success can become an idol.
- Money can become an idol.
- Sexual gratification can become an idol.
- Being right can become an idol.
- Looking good can become an idol.
- Comfort can become an idol.
- Being in control can become an idol.

And on and on it goes . . . the list of possible idols seems endless.

Anything you put your trust in to carry the day, other than God, is functioning as an idol in your life. Idols aren't typically in and of themselves "bad things." In fact, sometimes an idol is a good thing that becomes the main thing. Success, wealth, and power can all be good things—until they become the one thing. They are not automatically an idol. It is how you relate to them that determines whether you have them or if they have you. If anything in your life other than God is the "ultimate thing," that is an idol.

Keller adds this, "Contemporary idol worship continues today in the form of an addiction or devotion to money, career, sex, power, and anything people seek to give significance and satisfaction in life other than God."

Let's look at some of what God has to say about idols:

"All who fashion idols are nothing, and the things they delight in do not profit. Their witnesses neither see nor know, that they may be put to shame. Who fashions a god or casts an idol that is profitable for nothing? Behold, all his companions shall be put to shame, and the craftsmen are only human. Let them all assemble, let them stand forth. They shall be terrified; they shall be put to shame together." **Isaiah 44:9–11 (ESV)**

So, what does the Scripture above in Isaiah tell us are the ramifications of relying on idols?

- If we fashion idols, we are nothing. We are producing nothing worthwhile.
- We will reap no profit.
- We will experience shame.
- We will experience fear. In fact, we will be driven by fear.

Jerry loved soccer. He was good at soccer. He enjoyed soccer. Is soccer in and of itself a bad thing? Not at all. But for Jerry, success in soccer became all that really mattered to him. His thoughts and hopes were built around soccer. If you had asked him at the time if that were true, he might have denied it. But the way he was living revealed the reality of his idolatry and the destructive impact it was having on his wife and his heart.

His wife's commitment to their marriage was a catalyst for Jerry to start looking at things from a different perspective. And he realized that, for him, the wise choice was to go in a completely different direction. This is what the word repent means. It means to change your trajectory.

Jerry made the choices he needed to make to change his trajectory. And, in doing so, he is completely transforming the legacy of his life.

Jesus' first instructions to His followers were to *"repent, for the kingdom of heaven is at hand."* **(Matthew 3:2 ESV)** What he meant was to change your focus, change what matters most to you, change the trajectory you are on. Why do that? Because "the kingdom of heaven is at hand." Because making this commitment, an act of the will, opens up the fullness of what God has for us. It's the path to living in freedom, no longer weighed down by guilt and shame. It's the path He has prepared in all His wisdom and guidance, rather than us just blindly following our desires and notions.

WE HAVE A CHOICE . . . MOMENT BY MOMENT, DAY BY DAY. WE CHOOSE.

Deuteronomy so vividly encapsulates that choice:

"I call heaven and earth to testify against you today! I've set life and death before you today: both blessings and curses. Choose life, that it may be well with you—you and your children" **Deuteronomy 30:19 (ISV)**

God's path leads to life - the fullness of life. All else pales in comparison, and ultimately leads to death. The choice is yours. Don't go it alone. You may stumble. If you do, pick yourself up and go again. Moment by moment, we choose. And those choices determine the trajectory of your life.

PERSONAL STUDY NOTES

SCRIPTURE REFLECTION

**PERSONAL
STUDY
QUESTIONS**

1. What choices do you need to make today, at this point in time, to move you toward God's plan for your life?

2. Who in your life is living in such a way that you can gain inspiration and strength for your own journey? How can you engage them in a more purposeful and intentional way?

3. Have I addressed my "Next Steps" that I shared with my CORE group? If not, what is keeping me from stepping out and addressing it? What's my next step?

SCRIPTURE REFLECTION PRACTICE

We encourage you to consider the following Scripture passage over the course of this week in a prayerfully contemplative way.

This simple process will help you engage not only your mind but also your heart. Consider focusing this week on the same Scripture below (1 Peter 2:9–11) each day, using these principles:

- Be alert for a phrase or word that catches your attention. This could be in the form of a question on what it means or a new insight.
- Once during the week, read the verses aloud slowly.
- Once during the week, as you read the verses, pause along the way to use it to spark specific prayers to God.
- Finally, after reading the verses, pause to be thankful that *"it is God who works in you, both to will and to work for his good pleasure."* **Philippians 2:13 (ESV)**

SCRIPTURE REFLECTION FOR SESSION 4:
1 PETER 2:9–11 (NIV)

But you are a chosen people, a royal priesthood, a holy nation, God's special possession, that you may declare the praises of him who called you out of darkness into his wonderful light. Once you were not a people, but now you are the people of God; once you had not received mercy, but now you have received mercy. Dear friends, I urge you, as foreigners and exiles, to abstain from sinful desires, which wage war against your soul.

SCRIPTURE REFLECTION NOTES

SESSION

RELOAD
CLINT BRUCE

GROUP DISCUSSION GUIDE (90 MINUTES)

OPENING PRAYER
Surrender your time and heart to God's leading.

CHECK IN (20 MINUTES—2–3 MINUTES PER PERSON)
Be mindful of the need for everyone to have the opportunity to talk.
Take 1–2 minutes each time you share.

1. How has your week gone? Family? Work?

2. What kind of progress or challenges did you have with your "Next Steps" from last session?

3. How was your Personal Study and Scripture Reflection time this week? What is resonating? What is not working?

WATCH FILM (12 MINUTES)
Reload—Clint Bruce

GROUP DISCUSSION (45 MINUTES)

1. What part of Clint's story and sharing connected with you?

2. What "high, hard ridgelines" do you consider worth pursuing?

3. What new ground have you taken during this CORE series together?

NEXT STEPS (10 MINUTES)
Be mindful of the need for everyone to have an opportunity to talk. Take 2–3 minutes each. Take notes and pray for each other's "Next Steps" during the week. As always, keep everything confidential.

In light of today's discussion, what is one step you can take in your life or in your relationships this week? Something specific. Something measurable. Something the group can pray for during the week.

PERSONAL STUDY EXCERPT—READ OUT LOUD (3 MINUTES)
Clint says that for him, "Elite is just a little more than what you thought you could do before you get to excellent. And, living this way is a reflection of being a steward of your time."

Think of this in terms of your own purpose and calling in life. God has given you a new identity. My identity is not what others think about me; it's not what I think about me; it's what God believes about me. Out of this foundation He has an overarching purpose for all of us . . . to create flourishing in life everywhere we go . . . in every relationship, in every circumstance, in every exchange, in all things large and small.

God has given you a specific calling that is unique to you.

CLOSING PRAYER
Ask for God's guidance and strength during the week ahead.

CORE GROUP NOTES

🛡 PERSONAL STUDY

"Use your time for what matters." This is the final thing Clint Bruce says in his film.

As we discuss Clint Bruce's story, consider what he is saying about the areas of your life you have chosen to work on.

Ask yourself, "How can I actually apply this in my life?" Moving these insights into actual practices is the key. The goal moving forward is not to simply grow in more knowledge of what could be or should be. The aim is not to listen, be challenged, and then tuck the information away somewhere safe. Instead, actual and practical life-change is the objective of this session, these 5 weeks, and ultimately the objective of life. Like all that have gone before you, it means risk, failure, learning, and breakthrough.

Clint refers to something called a "ridgeline." A ridgeline is the highest edge of a mountain. It is the hardest place to get to, but it is also the place that provides the best protection and perspective. It's the place to celebrate the letting go of old ground and planning what it will take to advance into new ground. To get to the ridgeline, you have to make tremendous sacrifice and you must equip yourself with the tools and the friendships around you to make the climb. Through the rigorous process of traversing each ridgeline in your life, you will become more and more "elite."

Clint says that for him, "Elite is just a little more than what you thought you could do before you get to excellent. And, living this way is a reflection of being a steward of your time."

Think of this in terms of your own purpose and calling in life. God has given you a new identity. My identity is not what others think about me; it's not what I think about me; it's what God believes about me. Out of this foundation he has an overarching purpose for all of us . . .

to create flourishing in life everywhere we go . . . in every relationship, in every circumstance, in every exchange, in all things large and small.

God has given you a specific calling that is unique to you. It may take years and years for you to fully discover this, and that's okay. You go with what you are passionate about now, using the gifts you see God has given you, while staying open to God's leading as you move forward.

Think about your calling and purpose in light of what Clint said about stewardship. How we pursue our calling and purpose is a reflection of how we steward our time.

How much time do we have left? Not one of us knows the answer to this question. Pursuing elite is a reflection of urgency, because our days on this earth have an expiration date.

Clint draws the distinction between relaxing and reloading—the practice of how we choose to rest. Rest is a largely ignored spiritual discipline in our culture. The biblical concept of rest is much more than the absence of work. It's a day off. A vacation. The idea of observing "Sabbath," where we dedicate a day to unplug from responsibilities and spend that time with family and the community of faith is certainly rest. Practicing times of silence and solitude is rest.

When all that you do comes out of gratitude for Christ's love, it produces a supernatural rest unlike anything you could generate by yourself. This kind of rest allows you to begin the hard work of shedding the weight of needing to prove yourself and your worth.

So then, there remains a Sabbath rest for the people of God, for whoever has entered God's rest has also rested from his works as God did from his. **Hebrews 4:9–10 (ESV)**

Some may perceive rest as a lack of motivation or laziness. Maybe you've found yourself thinking, "I have too much to do. I have no time for this!" Perhaps you have heard yourself say, "Well, you don't

I FAILED MY WAY TO SUCCESS.

Thomas Edison

understand my schedule and responsibilities. I don't have time to rest." The fact is that rest is also action. It is a receptive, restorative action, rather than an assertive action. Our culture is all **about go, go, go.** We have lost the critical importance of rest as a preparation for effective action.

Rest, from a scriptural point of view, is a reloading with the understanding of Christ's finished work. Because of His death on our behalf, we are already His beloved children **(Ephesians 1:5–7)**.

It is out of this awareness that we can be infused with motivation to enter into His purpose and vision for our lives. It is a chance to reconnect to God and notice how we can be more fully present when we are in action.

Contemplative spiritual practices prepare us to reload and take action in a meaningful way. Contemplation on the truth and faith in action are joined at the hip. They are inseparable.

Reloading is getting grounded into what matters, in order to be prepared for what's next. Relaxing is different, as Clint describes it. Relaxing is seeking out rest for rest's sake, pleasure for pleasure's sake. It's self-focused. It's the end in and of itself. There is no ridgeline or specific vision attached to it.

Clint says, "David is such a great lesson in passion and authenticity and asking for grace.

"I don't know that you really know how to pray unless you read Psalms, because when you read Psalms, you're able to pray in a much more honest and raw way. David is perhaps the most encouraging biblical figure that we go back to because of his fallibility and how often he was a train wreck.

"Sometimes, many of us wonder if we're worth it. We often do these reckless things because we're just not sure if our actions or inactions have any real impact on anybody."

> **"DAVID WAS EVERY CRASH AND BURN THAT WE'VE SEEN IN THE LAST FIFTY YEARS IN SPORTS AND POLITICS AND BUSINESS ALL ROLLED UP IN ONE GUY. WHAT I THINK SAVED DAVID ALL THE TIME IS THAT AWARENESS OF WHO HE WAS AND THAT HE HAD BEEN PICKED AND WHY HE WAS THERE."**

We have this transcendent, amazing God who helps you know that you are worth it because he created you. Consistent times of reloading are moments that God reminds you of your worth. If all you do is go and go and go without stopping to reload, then you'll start believing that your worth is tied to your successes, or lack thereof.

- I can't seem to make my sales quota.
- I must be a horrible worker. I'm such a failure.
- I can't seem to find a job I actually enjoy; maybe I'll never find that. I probably don't deserve it anyway. Maybe that's an unrealistic expectation.
- Money is so tight each month. Why can't I provide in a way that takes all the stress off my family. What is wrong with me? I probably won't ever get this figured out.

Do any of these statements sound familiar?

You are NOT taking ridgelines to prove your worth. You take ridgelines because your worth has already been secured in Jesus. Now, you don't have to fear taking new ridgelines. You are free to climb. Clint continues,

"And I think that was David's great gift. It was the ability to just believe what God said when God talked about David. Every time he relaxed instead of reloading, he messed up with the absence of that ridgeline. The absence of that high hard thing that we're going to is where I made my most tremendous mistakes. This happens when I haven't clarified or remembered the high, hard ridgelines I'm going to, and also when I forget tying it all into the accountability of others."

Having a great marriage is a high, hard ridgeline. Raising kids to be healthy, responsible adults is a high, hard ridgeline. Creating flourishing in your work life is a high, hard ridgeline. Pursuing your purpose and calling without being distracted from it is a high, hard ridgeline. All of these require the same disciplines that Clint Bruce references in the context of his Navy Seal days.

He says, "Life is very much the series of picking a high ridgeline in it and then try, fail, fix, try again, and you do that over and over again. It's really hard to do that when you're wandering but if you're patrolling and if you're moving toward a target . . . if you're moving toward something that you decide is important to you and important to what you stand for . . . then that's just the process.

"What I've learned is you have to get to create those ridgelines.

"Those are all opportunities to put what you believe to work and to try and to fail and to fix and try again. It truly is all about whether you're willing to suffer. I don't like suffering for suffering's sake. There's got to be a reason that helps you pull through that resistance. And for me suffering has always been the barometer for someone's ability to do great things. Can they suffer, or will they suffer?"

When you suffer because life is not showing up the way you prefer or the way you intended, what are you going to do? Usually, we escape the suffering by trying to numb and distance ourselves, instead of reloading. Reloading embraces rest and reflection as we consider what isn't working, what's needed, what's next to go again.

This isn't just for Navy Seals in battle. This is for every single person. Regardless of your history, your personality, your temperament, your confidence, your IQ, or your savvy. Trying, failing, fixing, and trying again is the charge for each and every one of us. It's the charge for you.

This is how you make a dent in the world with your purpose and calling.

In fact, you could say this is at the very CORE of what we are about.

PERSONAL STUDY

Thank you for joining in with us on this CORE journey! Our deepest desire is for you to continue with a CORE group and lean into them as a resource and opportunity to serve and grow together. We have many more learning and action opportunities that you can utilize, and we hope they are an encouragement to you as you engage them.

Our desire is for you to be a powerful force for good . . .

- In your family
- In your church
- In your workplace
- In your city
- In the world

The greatest guidebook ever developed to do this is your Bible. The greatest and highest honor is to be called by God—not something we even remotely deserved but have been gifted by God's grace.

Now, let's do something about it! Use your time for what matters.

"My prayer is that when I die, all of hell rejoices that I am out of the fight." —C. S. Lewis

PERSONAL STUDY NOTES

REFLECTION

PERSONAL STUDY QUESTIONS

1. What high, hard ridgelines are you pursuing in your life?

2. What new ground have you taken in the last five weeks?

3. What is wanted and needed moving forward?

4. What's next for your CORE group? Visit us on our web site, **coreunites.com**, to get the latest resources to support your group in your journey together. You can also follow us on social media **@coreunites**.

SCRIPTURE REFLECTION PRACTICE

We encourage you to consider the following Scripture passage over the course of this week in a prayerfully contemplative way. This simple process will help you engage not only your mind but also your heart. Consider focusing this week on the same Scripture below (Philippians 3:8–12) each day, using these principles:

- Be alert for a phrase or word that catches your attention. This could be in the form of a question on what it means or a new insight.
- Once during the week, read the verses aloud slowly.
- Once during the week, as you read the verses, pause along the way to use it to spark specific prayers to God.
- Finally, after reading the verses, pause to be thankful that *"it is God who works in you, both to will and to work for his good pleasure."* **Philippians 2:13 (ESV)**

SCRIPTURE REFLECTION FOR SESSION 5: PHILIPPIANS 3:8–12 (ESV)

Indeed, I count everything as loss because of the surpassing worth of knowing Christ Jesus my Lord. For his sake I have suffered the loss of all things and count them as rubbish, in order that I may gain Christ and be found in him, not having a righteousness of my own that comes from the law, but that which comes through faith in Christ, the righteousness from God that depends on faith—that I may know him and the power of his resurrection, and may share his sufferings, becoming like him in his death, that by any means possible I may attain the resurrection from the dead.

Not that I have already obtained this or am already perfect, but I press on to make it my own, because Christ Jesus has made me his own.

What Paul is describing here is the highest ridgeline you can ever pursue!

SCRIPTURE REFLECTION NOTES

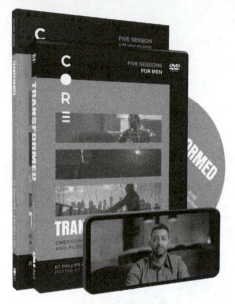

EMBRACING OUR TRUE IDENTITY AND PURPOSE

God never designed us to just figure things out on our own. When Jesus came to earth to start a revolution, he did so by gathering a small band of ordinary men around him. These men had unique backgrounds, diverse occupations, and individual personalities. Jesus orchestrated learning environments as they worked alongside each other that changed them into the most powerful, transformative community in the history of the world. Together, they went from self-centered individuals to united powerhouses.

Study Guide: 9780310131755
DVD with Free Streaming Access: 9780310131779

The goal of the CORE studies is set men on a similar journey that will transform them and their group into this type of community. Each study features five real-life stories of men who have faced real-life challenges and discovered transformation, redemption, restoration, purpose, and identity. These stories serve as a catalyst for men to start being real about their own stories and realize they are not alone in the struggle. In turn, this opens them up to getting the encouragement necessary to engage in life proactively.

There has never been a more critical need to equip men with the tools to win the battles over their hearts and futures. CORE gives them the ability to create spaces where they can show up as they are without judgment, be open about their struggles, and find freedom to discover who God says they are. They will be invited to step out of shame and isolation and encouraged to step into their God-given purpose.

This study features an introduction from Jeremy Affeldt and stories from well-known speakers on the topics of identity, transformation, brotherhood, choices, and renewal.

Available now at your favorite bookstore,
or streaming video on StudyGateway.com.

CORE

CORE creates space where men can be real.
A space where they are no longer alone in facing
their struggles or pursuing their dreams.

Space where they can discover, in community,
what the scriptures say who they really are
and what they were made for.

WHAT'S NEXT?

For additional series and resources for leaders
go to **coreunites.com/whatsnext**

A PROVEN PATHWAY TO EXPERIENCE IDENTITY, BROTHERHOOD, AND TRANSFORMATION

God longs for you to be transformed into his image, and one of the most effective methods of becoming like Christ is to be in community with like-minded brothers. In this five-session video Bible study, you will hear stories from six well-known men who have faced real-life challenges and renewed their minds through God's Word and the brotherhood of other men.

There has never been a more critical time to be equipped with the tools you need to win the battle over your heart and future. This CORE study will give you and the other men in your group the space to show up just as you are without judgment, be open about your struggles with each other, and find freedom to discover who God says you are. You will be invited to step out of shame and isolation and encouraged to step into your God-given purpose!

This study guide features group discussion questions, personal study, and Scripture reflection.

Sessions include:

1. Identity (with Propaganda)
2. Transformation (with Willie Alfonso)
3. Brotherhood (with The Acho Brothers)
4. Choices (with Jerry Quiroz)
5. Reload (with Clint Bruce)

Designed for use with the *Transformed Video Study* digital video or DVD, sold separately.

RT PHILLIPS served as a pastor for twenty years. He was the first President of Promise Keepers, the visionary leader for Stand in the Gap, and contributing author of the best-selling *Seven Promises of a Promise Keeper*.

TIM PHILLIPS brings a strategic and passionate approach to helping create brotherhood communities that help turn weakness into strength, and authenticity into confident purpose.

Cover design by CORE
Original package design © 2020 Zondervan

RELIGION / Christian Living / Men's Interests
USD $13.99 / CAD $17.50
ISBN 978-0-310-13175-5

51399

9 780310 131755

ZONDERVAN®
.com

C O R E